*Jus*

# DAUGHTER

Illustrated by

*Douglas Hall*

A.R.C.A.

Selected by Anne Rose

BROCKHAMPTON PRESS

Little Girl
Sweet and small
Cock does crow
So do you.
Merry voice
Infant noise
Merrily Merrily to welcome in the Year.

William Blake, *Songs of Innocence*

As is the mother, so is her daughter.

*Ezekiel*, XVI:44

If I should ever by chance grow rich
I'll buy Codham, Cockridden, and Childerditch.
Roses, Pyrgo, and Lapwater,
And let them all to my elder daughter.

Edward Thomas, *If I Should Ever by Chance*

Monday's child is fair of face,
Tuesday's child is full of grace,
Wednesday's child is full of woe,
Thursday's child has far to go,
Friday's child is loving and giving,
Saturday's child works hard for a living,
But the child that is born on the Sabbath day,
Is merry, and happy, and bright, and gay.

English proverb

I have so many anxieties about her growing up. I just hope she will get a chance to grow up. I hope there is a world for her to grow up in. I watch the news and think, 'They're going to blow up the world, just when I've got this little peach here.'
Meryl Streep

Angels at the foot,
And Angels at the head,
And like a curly little lamb
My pretty babe in bed.
Christina Rossetti

To my daughter Leonora without whose never-failing sympathy and encouragement this book would have been finished in half the time.
P. G. Wodehouse, dedication in *The Heart of a Goof*

O fairer daughter of a fair mother.
Horace, *Odes*

What a mother sings to the cradle
goes all the way to the coffin.
Henry Beecher Ward

Children are the anchors that hold a mother to life.
Sophocles

A son is a son till he gets him a wife,
But a daughter's a daughter the rest of your life.
Dinah Marie Craik

There was a little girl
Who had a little curl
Right in the middle of her forehead;
And when she was good
She was very, very good,
But when she was bad she was horrid.
Henry Wadsworth Longfellow

The father of a daughter, especially one in her teens, will find that she doesn't like to be seen walking with him on the street. In fact, she will often ask him to walk a few paces behind.
Bill Cosby, *Fatherhood*

A daughter is an embarrassing
and ticklish possession.

Menander, *Perinthis*

Give a little love to a child, and you get a great
deal back.
John Ruskin

By the short of Gitche Gumee,
By the shining Big-Sea-Water,
Stood the wigwam of Nokomis,
  Daughter of the Moon, Nokomis.
    Henry Wadsworth Longfellow,
      *The Song of Hiawatha*

Children when they are little make
  parents fools, when great, mad.
    Samuel Richardson

Unless you can muse in a crowd all day
On the absent face that fixed you;
Unless you can love, as the angels may,
With the breadth of heaven betwixt you;
Unless you can dream that his faith is fast,
Through behoving and unbehoving;
Unless you can die when the dream is past —
Oh, never call it loving!

Elizabeth Barrett Browning, *A Woman's Shortcomings*

Love seeketh not itself to please,
Nor for itself hath any care,
But for another gives its ease,
And builds a heaven
in hell's despair.
William Blake

One is not born a woman,
one becomes one.
Simone de Beauvoir, *The Second Sex*

Mother love, particularly in America, is a highly
respected and much publicized emotion and when
exacerbated by gin and bourbon it can become
extremely formidable.
Noel Coward

A teenage daughter is easier to love in retrospect.
Jan du Plessis

We are all born for love; it is the principle of
existence and its only end.
Benjamin Disraeli

I'd been handed twenty-odd years wrapped up in this bundle, and hoped to see her grow, learn to totter, to run into the garden, run back, and call this place home. But I realized from these beginnings that I'd got a daughter whose life was already separate from mine, whose will already followed its own direction. ... She was a child of herself and would be what she was, I was merely the keeper of her temporary helplessness.

Laurie Lee, *Two Women*

Oh, she was good as she was fair!
None — none on earth above her!
As pure in thought as angels are,
To know her is to love her.

Samuel Rogers

If only youth had the knowledge; if only age had
the strength.

Henri Estienne

A child should always say what's true,
And speak when she is spoken to,
And behave mannerly at table:
At least as far as she is able.

Robert Louis Stevenson

Know you what it is to be a child? ... It is to
believe in love, to believe in loveliness ... it is to be
so little that the elves can reach to whisper in
your ear ... for each child has its fairy godmother
in his own soul.

Francis Thompson

It is customary, but I think it is
a mistake, to speak of happy childhood.
Children are often over-anxious and
acutely sensitive. Man ought to be man
and master of his fate; but children are
at the mercy of those around them.

Sir John Lubbock

One's prime is elusive. You little girls, when you grow up, must be on the alert to recognize your prime at whatever time of your life it may occur.
Muriel Spark, *The Prime of Miss Jean Brodie*

Child of the pure unclouded brow
And dreaming eyes of wonder!
Lewis Carroll, *Through the Looking-Glass*

- It matters not how long we live, but how.
P. J. Bailey

Oh, for the simple life,
For tents and starry skies!
Israel Zangwill

Nothing in life is more wonderful than faith — the
one great moving force which we can neither
weight in the balance nor test in the crucible.
Sir William Osler

I always found my daughters' beaux
Invisible as the emperor's clothes.
Ogden Nash

Selfishness is one of the qualities apt to inspire
love. This might be thought out at great length.
Nathaniel Hawthorne

Children are a poor man's riches.
Thomas Fuller

A blessing upon your tallest grass,
A blessing upon your fruitful partner,
A blessing upon your growing sons,
Upon your growing daughters.
Celtic blessing

A daughter reminds you of all the things you had
forgotten about being young. Good and bad.
Maeve O'Reilly

Don't put your daughter on the stage,
Mrs Worthington.
Noel Coward, *Mrs Worthington*

This then was my daughter, born in the autumn ...
lying purple and dented like a little bruised plum.
She was of course just an ordinary miracle ...
Laurie Lee, *Two Women*

At the moment that a boy of thirteen is turning
towards girls, a girl of thirteen is turning on her
mother. This girl can get rather unreasonable,
often saying such comical things as, 'Listen, this is
my life!'
Bill Cosby, *Fatherhood*

It is a beauteous evening, calm and free,
The holy time is quiet as a Nun
Breathless with adoration; the broad sun
Is sinking down in its tranquillity;
The gentleness of heaven broods o'er the Sea:
Listen! the mighty Being is awake,
And doth with his eternal motion make
A sound like thunder — everlastingly.
Dear Child! dear Girl! that walkest with me here,
If thou appear untouched by solemn thought,
Thy nature is not therefore less divine:
Thou liest in Abraham's bosom all the year;
And worshipp'st at the Temple's inner shrine,
God being with thee when we know it not.
William Wordsworth

What are little girls made of?
What are little girls made of?
Sugar and spice
And all things nice,
That's what little girls are made of.

Traditional

The supreme happiness of life is the conviction
that we are loved.

Victor Hugo

She is pretty to walk with,
And witty to walk with,
And pleasant to think on.

Sir John Suckling

I am struck, not for the first time, by her unique blend of innocence and knowledge ... Always at such moments she reminds me of someone ... But today I see for the first time who it is she reminds me of: it's me.

Carol Shields, *Small Ceremonies*

Marrying off your daughter is a piece of business you may expect to do only once in a lifetime, and, bearing in mind that none of the losses are recoverable later, you should approach the matter with extreme caution.

Ihara Saikaku, Japanese novelist

... Can you look at her and recall the cost and say
it was truly worth it?
That you did right? Ah, how can I say?
How can I possibly say? My youngest daughter,
like my eldest daughter, like any loved and
wanted child, was, is, worth anything
and everything, is more precious than rubies.
There is no way you can make up a balance sheet,
weigh this against that on some scale.

Susan Hill, *Family*

My daughter, how do I rejoice! for thy children
        flock around like the gay fishes on
            the wave, when the cold moon
                drinks the dew ...

William Blake,

*Ethinthus, Queen of Waters*

Youth is a wonderful thing. What a crime to waste it on children.

George Bernard Shaw

Sole daughter of my house and heart.

Lord Byron, *Childe Harold's Pilgrimage*

Would'st be happy, little child,
Be thou innocent and mild:
Like the patient lamb and dove,
Full of meekness, full of love;
Modestly thy looks compose,
Sweet and blushing like the rose.

Anonymous, *To Theodora*

Fame is rot; daughters are the thing.

Sir James Barrie, *Dear Brutus II*

My fairest child, I have no song to give you;
  No lark could pipe to skies so dull and grey:
Yet, ere we part, one lesson I can leave you
  For every day.

Be good, sweet maid, and let who will be clever;
  Do noble things, not dream them, all day long;
And so make life, death, and that vast forever
  One grand sweet song.

Charles Kingsley, *A Farewell*

Three daughters is no laughing matter.

Jewish proverb

Thank God for my beautiful daughter.
She has far surpassed her brothers in the
phone-call department. Girls often do.
Lauren Bacall, *Now*

Love me — I love you,
  Love me, my baby;
Sing it high, sing it low
  Sing it as may be.

Mother's arms under you;
  Her eyes above you;
Sing it high, sing it low,
  Love me — I love you.
Christina Rossetti, *Love Me - I Love You*

I see her sleeping there ... a princess on her crisp
white sheets.
Will she need me tomorrow?
Kitty Browne

Yes little girls are wonderful
a gift from God above
They're little angels sent to earth
a symbol of His love.
Anonymous

Thank heaven for little girls!
Alan Jay Lerner

I love thee, Baby! for thine own sweet sake;
Those azure eyes, that faintly dimpled cheek,
Thy tender frame, so eloquently weak,
Love in the sternest heart of hate might wake;
Percy Bysshe Shelley, *To Ianthe*

A man can deceive his fiancée or his
mistress as much as he likes, and in
the eyes of a woman he loves, an
ass may pass for a philosopher,
but a daughter is a different
matter.
Anton Chekhov

But where's the song
  for our small dear,
With her quaint voice and
her quick ear,
To sing — for dreamland things
to hear —
And hush herself to sleep?
Ford Madox Ford, *The Unwritten Song*

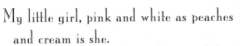

My little girl, pink and white as peaches
  and cream is she.
My little girl is half again as nice as girls are
  meant to be.
Oscar Hammerstein

Mother may I go and bathe?
Yes, my darling daughter.
Hang your clothes on yonder tree,
But don't go near the water.

Anonymous

I need to be as understood as much in motherhood
as I ever did in daughterdom.

Lauren Bacall, *Now*

I have a small daughter called Cleis, who is like a
golden flower, but I wouldn't take all Croesus'
kingdom with love thrown in, for her.

Sappho

Little one,
making you
has centred my lopsided life.
Erica Jong

Love me always and forever, my existence
depends on it ... as I told you the other day
you are all my joy and all my sorrow.
What remains of my life is overshadowed
by grief when I consider how much of it
will be spent far from you.
Madame de Sevigné

A little girl can be sweeter (and badder) oftener than anyone else in the world. She can jitter around, and stomp, and make funny noises that frazzle your nerves, yet just when you open your mouth she stands there demure with that special look in her eyes. A girl is Innocence playing in the mud. Beauty standing on its head, and Motherhood dragging a doll by the foot.

Alan Beck

How can one say no to a child? How can one be anything but a slave to one's own flesh and blood?

Henry Miller

I love you not only for what you are, but for what
I am when I am with you.
I love you not only for what you have made of
yourself, but for what you are making of me.
I love you because you have done more than
anyone could have done to make me good, and more
than any fate could have done to make me happy.
You have done it by being yourself.
Anonymous

The best moments of a visit are those which again
and again postpone its close.
Jean Paul Richter

Where did you come from, baby dear?
Out of the everywhere into here.
George Macdonald, *At the Back of the North Wind*

◈

Love is like the wild rose-briar;
Friendship like the holly-tree.
The holly is dark when the rose-briar blooms,
but which will bloom most constantly?
Emily Brontë

◈

Oh, the comfort, the inexpressible comfort,
of feeling safe with a person ...
George Eliot

There's only one pretty child in the world,
and every mother has it.

Proverb

❖

Softly, in the dusk, a woman is singing to
me;
Taking me back down the vista of years, till
I see
A child sitting under the piano, in the
boom of the tingling strings
And pressing the small, poised feet of a
mother who smiles as she sings.

D. H. Lawrence, *Piano*

I want someone to laugh with me, someone to
be grave with me, someone to please me and
help my discrimination with ... her own
remark, and at times, no doubt, to admire my
acuteness and penetration.
Robert Burns

Blessed be childhood, which brings down
something of heaven into the midst of our
rough earthliness.
Henri Frederic Amiel

O Child beside the Waterfall
what songs without a word
rise from those waters like the call
only a heart has heard
the Joy, the Joy in all things
rise whistling like a bird.

O Child beside the Waterfall
I see you standing there
with waterdrops and fireflies
and hummingbirds in the air
all singing praise of paradise
paradise everywhere.

George Barker, *O Child Beside the Waterfall*

My daughter! O my ducats! O my daughter!
... O my Christian ducats!
Justice — the law — my ducats and my daughter!
William Shakespeare, *The Merchant of Venice*

Her manipulations of me began before she could speak, and I was too fond to withstand them. Lying on a coloured blanket in the morning, rigid with expectation, waiting for me to carry her round the garden. If anyone else approached her, she'd kick and howl, but when I bent over her, and wrapped her up, she'd relax with a complacent sigh.

Laurie Lee, *Two Women*

My heart is like a singing bird
Whose nest is in a water'd shoot
My heart is like an apple tree
Whose boughs are bent with thickest fruit;
My heart is like a rainbow shell
That paddles in a halcyon sea;
My heart is gladder than all these
Because my love is come to me.

Christina Rossetti

To love and to be loved is the greatest happiness of existence.
Sydney Smith

A child enters your home and for the next twenty years makes so much noise you can hardly stand it. The child departs, leaving the house so silent you think you are going mad.
John Andrew Holmes

What do we live for, if it is not to make life less difficult for each other?
George Eliot

She is inventive, original, and takes what she
wants from life — including many of her mother's
clothes. When she comes into a room she expects
something to happen and, if it doesn't, she takes
steps to see that it does.
Rachel Billington, *The Great Umbilical*

I have done little with my life,
created nothing wonderful,
given no new knowledge to the world.
But I am content.
I have given it a daughter.
Most wonderful. Most wise.
Maya V. Patel

Give me a girl at an impressionable age, and she
is mine for life.
Muriel Spark, *The Prime of Miss Jean Brodie*

Where did you come from, baby dear?
Out of the everywhere into here.
George Macdonald, *At the Back of the North Wind*

Behold the child, by nature's kindly law,
Pleased with a rattle, tickled with a straw.
Alexander Pope, *Essays on Man*

Love is a passion that hath friends in a garrison.
George Savile, *Advice to a Daughter*

Marrying off your daughter is a piece of business
you may expect to do only once in a lifetime, and,
bearing in mind that none of the losses are
recoverable later, you should approach the matter
with extreme caution.
Ihara Saikaku

I am the daughter of my father's house,
William Shakespeare, *Twelfth Night*

Just yesterday, God,
she was a tiny thing,
squirming, helpless and loud,
in her eyelet trimmed,
oak-barred boudoir.
Now look at her:
like some caricatured Amazon Goddess,
she flings about dolls and balls
and books,
then cheers in wild abandon.
Jayne Jaudon Ferror,
'Growing Pains', A New Mother's Thoughts

# Acknowledgements:

The Publishers wish to thank everyone who gave permission to reproduce the quotes in this book. Every effort has been made to contact the copyright holders, but in the event that an oversight has occurred, the publishers would be delighted to rectify any omissions in future editions of this book. Children's quotes printed courtesy of Herne Hill School, Hannah Rough and Kingfisher County Primary School; *The Heart of a Goof*, P.G. Wodehouse, Hutchinson; *Ordinary Miracles*, Erica Jong, reprinted courtesy of HarperCollins Publishers Ltd; *Two Women*, Laurie Lee © Laurie Lee, reprinted courtesy of Peters, Fraser & Dunlop Group, Ltd.; *Verses from 1929 On* © Ogden Nash, reprinted courtesy of Curtis Brown Ltd, New York, first appeared in *The New Yorker*; *Fatherhood*, *Time Flies* and *Childhood*, Bill Cosby, reprinted courtesy of Doubleday, a division of Transworld Publishers; *Family*, Susan Hill, reprinted courtesy of Penguin Books; *The Great Umbilical*, by Rachel Billington, reprinted courtesy of David Higham Associates Ltd.; *Mrs Worthington*, Noel Coward, Jonathan Cape, part of Random House; *Small Ceremonies*, Carol Shields, Fourth Estate; J.M Barrie, reprinted courtesy of Great Ormond Street Hospital; *The Unwritten Song*, Ford Madox Ford, Random House UK Limited; 'Growing Pains', in *A New Mother's Thoughts*, Jayne Jaudon Ferror, reprinted courtesy of Pocket Books, a division of Simon & Schuster Inc.